NOBODY GOES TO HEAVEN KICKING AND SCREAMING

Nobody Goes To Heaven Kicking And Screaming
Copyright © 2023 by Kimmy Littlejohn-Clark

Published in the United States of America
ISBN   Paperback: 978-1-960629-56-2
ISBN   eBook: 978-1-960629-57-9

All rights reserved. No part of this publication may be reproduced, stored in a retrieval system or transmitted in any way by any means, electronic, mechanical, photocopy, recording or otherwise without the prior permission of the author except as provided by USA copyright law.

The opinions expressed by the author are not necessarily those of ReadersMagnet, LLC.

ReadersMagnet, LLC
10620 Treena Street, Suite 230 | San Diego, California, 92131 USA
1.619. 354. 2643 | www.readersmagnet.com

Book design copyright © 2023 by ReadersMagnet, LLC. All rights reserved.

Cover design by Kent Gabutin
Interior design by Daniel Lopez

NOBODY GOES TO HEAVEN KICKING AND SCREAMING

Kimmy Littlejohn-Clark

ReadersMagnet, LLC

TABLE OF CONTENTS

CHAPTER 1:	WHY SUCH A TITLE?..	1
CHAPTER 2:	I HOPE...	3
CHAPTER 3:	THEY MEET HIM DAILY	6
CHAPTER 4:	STAY WOKE...	9
CHAPTER 5:	TO KNOW HIM IS TO LOVE HIM	12
CHAPTER 6	TOMORROW IS PROMISED.........................	15
CHAPTER 7:	LET ME BE SPIRITUAL	18
CHAPTER 8:	LAST CALL FOR SALVATION	20

CHAPTER 1

Why Such A Title?

I'm sure you're wondering what made me think of a title like this. Well, since I've been in relationship with the Lord I'm always imagining how I'll enter heaven. I have also witnessed people transition smoothly. I'm referring to Saints. Revelation 14:13(NLT) says And I heard a voice from heaven saying, "Write this down: Blessed are those who die in the Lord from now on. Yes, says the Spirit, they are blessed indeed, for they will rest from their hard work, for their good deeds follow them!"

My thoughts take me to the story of Elijah. He didn't die, but was taken up to heaven in a whirlwind. In your quiet time with the Lord read if you will. 2 Kings 2:1-17(ESV). Elijah didn't tell him it was his time to go. Elisha is the one who cried out. Perhaps he cried out because he wasn't ready for Elijah to go. Just like we do when our family or friends die. Are we ever ready for anyone to go? 9 times out of 10 the answer is no.

The older I get I usually end up in a conversation regarding death. It's a discussion many don't want to have. Even as I write this people are transitioning to that great city of heaven or to a never ending hellfire.

The most popular sayings are "heaven has gained an angel", "they went to glory" or they earned their wings. Hmmm… is there such a thing? There are several scriptures on wings. From my understanding when we die nothing in the Bible supports that when we get to heaven we'll receive wings.

So it looks like I'll wait until I get there to see. I'm sure heaven will be beyond my most vast imagination, but for now I will focus on scripture about rewards ex: Revelation 22:12 and Philippians 3:14.

There's so much to see in heaven I'm just excited about all that is to come.

CHAPTER 2

I Hope

We all have said more than once the words "I hope". "I hope I get a raise", "I hope my marriage lasts", "I hope my child gets their life together". The list goes on when it comes to saying "I hope".

I want to talk about the word hope when it comes to God. When we surrender our heart to salvation we gain all the hope we will ever need. 1 Peter 1:13(NIV) reminds us to set your hope on the grace to be brought to you. It also tells us to be fully sober.

We know Jesus is gonna return for his bride so we can easily say "I hope he comes soon". The world has taken a turn for the worse. Take a look at 2 Timothy 3:1 (KJV). I actually do "hope" he comes soon.

When I read scriptures like Hebrew 10:23(NIV), Isaiah 40:31(NIV), Psalm 33:22(NIV) I smile. We should wake up daily and remember to put our hope in the Lord. He is so powerful and is able to soothe us. He loves us even when we're difficult and nobody else wants to love us. The greatest demonstration of his love for us is John 3:16(NIV). Therefore, no child of God should walk around saying "I hope" God loves me.

Sinners are the only ones who have no hope. Please know the difference.

People have heavy hearts and their minds are cluttered. They are sleepless and hopeless. Death for a sinner doesn't end well (2 Thessalonians 1:8-9 ESV). It's horrible and to think the fire will never be quenched.

When one dies in the Lord and leaves their loved ones behind to grieve it ends differently. All who are left behind (who are in the Lord) can freely grieve with hope. One day they will be reunited. I still grieve the loss of my baby boy Chancz. But I grieve with hope. This is why I told him "see you later" 1 Thessalonians 4:13 (NLT). That scripture encourages my soul every time I read it.

I'm encouraging whomever is reading this now to remember death in the Lord will never leave you hopeless.

CHAPTER 3

They Meet Him Daily

I grew up seeing mommy and daddy having Bible time together (he's been in heaven 25 yrs. now). I would often see them on their knees in their bedroom praying. Mommy meets the Lord daily. At the kitchen table is where she communes with The Lord. She sits with her magnifying glass to read and pray. She has truly shown me there's no place off limits for prayer. I laughed at her and daddy back in the day and thought look at those cheese balls. Who does all of this reading and praying when I can run the streets. LOL

Years later here I am a cheese ball too.

She's definitely the mother I needed. She's up in age and so admires and worships the creator. One of her favorite scripture is Ecclesiastes 12:1(NKJV)

Remember now your creator in the days of your youth, before the difficult days come and the years draw near when you say I have no pleasure in them. I now grasp what that means.

It's so important to carve out time with the Lord. You can learn something new all the time. At her age she's still learning and is amazed. Going back to that scripture helps me understand how the older soldiers (or seasoned saints) don't panic on difficult days. They've traveled down the road younger soldiers are on and have seen his mighty hand. They may worry a little, but have come too far to panic… I imagine saints before me would probably hear the Lord say "Is there anything too hard for me?" Jeremiah 32:27(ESV).

The devil loves to see us doubting.

My aunt Doris also meets with him daily and says nobody can tell her that coffee and the word (Bible) ain't anointed. LOL I couldn't agree more. I've watched her be calm in the midst of trouble. She has plenty of battle scars from all she has gone through in her walk. Early on in my walk I remember her asking me to pray for her… I was caught off guard and nervous. She saw something in me that I didn't see and encouraged me to walk until I saw it. It is still paying off to this day. Now at 52 when she needs me to pray I can do it with boldness. Thank you Lord for my wonderful Aunt.

So what is my message to you right now? It doesn't matter where you meet Jesus in prayer, worship or precious time in his word. I've met with him in the car, on the beach, and lying in bed. Simply meet with him daily.

CHAPTER 4

Stay Woke

There's a popular saying that I hear young people say all the time. "stay woke". I know when they find out about something they feel nobody really knows they say it.

I want to say first of all everyone ain't woke. When I say this I mean if you're unsaved not only are you not woke, scripture says you're walking dead. Yes, you're dead in your trespasses (Ephesians 2:1 AMP). Your spirit is literally dead. You can't see things the Lord's way because you're of the world (John 14:17 AMP).

The word of God is not going to make sense to you. Read 1 Corinthians 1:18(NLT). I've shared the good news(witnessed) to people and some have given me strange looks. After we part ways I've said to myself

I bet they're calling me crazy or stupid. However, I can't let the moment be lost. This is the reason I pray to the Lord and ask him to prompt me when the light is green. I say Lord give me the words to say... and when I need to shut up make me speechless.

The Holy Spirit surely has done what I've asked. I am grateful because I don't want to be in flesh mode. (Gal 5:16 HCSB) It can easily happen too... What do I mean by this? I don't want to talk too much just to sound deep. My goal is to please God and bring him glory.

It's been 2 years since the Covid19 pandemic... Covid is still hanging around. People are sick, hurt, fearful, you name it. And with all that's going on they're missing a Savior. Never had I witnessed a pandemic until 2020. I feel it helped me draw closer to Him. It has reminded me he's still saving souls and healing the sick. He hasn't been slacking with healing power, or deaf when his name is called.

So if everyone ain't woke I'll once again tell you now's the time to "wake up"! It's all in a confession of faith Romans 10:9(NIV). Those verses will never grow old or be deleted.

I'd like to believe 100% God is talking to people of faith (Saints) when he says what's in Romans 13:1 (AMP) because only his people can hear or see.

So for someone who may read this I pray you run to the altar with a confession of faith and receive Jesus as Lord and Savior. I promise your vision and your hearing will be instant. You will have new eyes and ears. You'll be able to say "I'm woke"!

CHAPTER 5

To Know Him Is To Love Him

Why not serve a God who is sovereign and perfect? His thoughts about us are perfect.

I believe one of the reasons people have a hard time serving God is because they have unanswered questions. I don't claim to be right about everything, but truth be told I still have unanswered questions.

I refuse to let it stop me from living for him. It's not worth it to spend forever in hell because of things I can't understand. Hell is too long and forever for me. I'm pretty sure per scripture God doesn't mind questions. He's loving and not willing that any should perish. He's also patient.

Bottom line is nobody will have an excuse on judgment day (2 Peter 3:9 NKJV). The more I walk with him the more my love has grown.

Getting to know him is exciting. God is not boring. His love for us is so strong. So strong he sent his only son to the cross. This is why I say "to know him is to love him". John 15:9(NIV) talks about how the father (God) loves Jesus the son and this is why he loves us.

We can rely on God's love… if nobody else loves us, we can be 100% sure his love is real. We live in perilous times and many people feel unloved and unwanted. God not only wants to love us, but he wants to save our souls.

Love is something that can come and go in your life. Except God's love is unfailing. The entire Psalm 136 says it over and over "his love endures forever. I'm glad with all the people in the world he has enough love to go around. We can get to know him and fall in love. It's safe to love him (Proverb 18:10 (NKJV). Love is a risk, but not with God. I took a chance on love with God 25 years ago. I have no regrets. Psalm118:8(KJV) we can trust him better than we can trust man.

I try to remember to run to God with all my problems and lay them at his feet. He soothes me and I love to talk his ears off. LOL

I admonish you to bask in his presence… you'll feel loved and safe. Psalm 86:5(NLT) says his heart is full.

CHAPTER 6

Tomorrow Is Promised

We have been taught to say "tomorrow is not promised". When you read scripture it seems to be a bad quote. God does promise us things in the Bible. Tomorrow (numbered days) are one of them.

I would like to discuss the conditions when it comes to being promised tomorrow.

Psalm 90:10(NIV) talks about strength. He has his own reason for saying this. And I'd love to know more about this when I behold his face. Before this scripture, let's go with what may be the main condition... "Obedience". Exodus 20:12(NKJV) says he promises long life if you obey your father and mother. He really didn't give us too hard of a task. Simply honor your parents and you'll live a long life.

In another scripture he says he'll give us 70 years or 80 if we have strength. God knows how much strength we have to get up and move around daily. So not even a doctor can determine how long one lives. God has all power.

Nothing seems more beautiful than to live a life with God on earth then transition to heaven to live again in His kingdom.

So there you have it… if you obey, you get a long life. It also depends on your strength.

The Lord wants us to live Godly and walk in obedience to his will and way. Honestly, in my own walk my desire to obey is improving. It's not always easy because flesh gets in the way. That's why you have to tell your flesh to die daily (Matthew 16:24 NIV).

I tell God all the time what I want and desire. Then I tell him if it's not his will then I don't want it. It took years for me to get to this level of faith. I wanted EVERYTHING I prayed for and about to come to pass. LOL

When I was pregnant it didn't cross my mind that my infant son Chancz was only promised 43 days. I felt disappointed because I prayed over him in that hospital and exercised my faith until the bitter end. I was so mad at God, but here I am 10 years (after Chancz died) saying God knows how many "tomorrows" are promised to every human being in the world (Job 14:5). All saints get to see "tomorrow" whether it be on earth or in heaven. If I don't wake up on earth my new "tomorrow" will start in heaven. Will your tomorrow be in Heaven or hell?

CHAPTER 7

Let Me Be Spiritual

You may get a happily ever after in a marriage on earth. However, if you're not married to Jesus you won't have a happily ever after with him in heaven.

Salvation saves you from sins, but it's a marriage. That's why he refers to the church as his bride (Rev 19:7-9 NIV). You have to nurture your walk daily. James 4:8(NIV) says come near to God and he will come near to you. I didn't quote the rest of the scripture as I am trying to make my point about nurturing your walk. Isaiah 26:3(NIV) can remind you of how you need to keep your mind on him. By spending time with him and diving in his word you will experience peace. Don't just get saved just to say you're saved.

Your growth in the Lord will help you become more spiritual. The Lord wants us to be more like him and he doesn't promote us to be religious. The Scribes and Pharisees were religious and caught up in the wrong things… you see how that turned out for them (Mat 5:20 NLT).

Looking back on my life and seeing all the roads I turned on. Whew! I experienced turbulence, because of choices I made.

Thank the Lord for prayers of the righteous. I'm grateful for that ONE road called the "straight and narrow" (Matt 7:13-14NIV). My encouragement to saints is to ask the Lord to help you be spiritual.

CHAPTER 8

Last Call For Salvation

I believe who you're married to plays a great role in your final destination. Friendship circles too.

The best choice I ever made was to accept Jesus as my Lord and Savior. I try to be intentional with time in the word and prayer… it keeps me encouraged.

I was so fearful in my "pre Jesus days" I didn't want to be around anyone who talked about death and hell. Yikes! Losing our infant son in 43 days forever changed my way of thinking (as a saint). I once felt like nobody should die unless they were old and wrinkled. The Lord gives specific details on life and death and I'm glad I chose life, life eternal.(Joshua 24:14-15 ESV) I don't have to leave this world kicking and screaming since I chose Jesus.

I've witnessed people who chose death and if I let my mind go back in time they kicked and screamed on their way out. After working a shift and seeing someone die out of Christ I would be scared to go to sleep sometimes. Fear didn't last long as the devil distracted me and I got back to my usual foolishness back in the day.

I am also glad to have seen people pass away calm and with smiles on their faces as they fell into their heavenly sleep. Now I don't want anyone thinking saints don't ever scream when they die . After all, some saints die in plane crashes, car accidents, etc.

Even in the Old Testament I can believe saints who were killed by lions or stoned to death screamed.... with the exception of Stephen (read Acts 7:54-60 NIV). If you read 1 Kings 13 or 1 Kings 20 the Lord's wrath came and lions had someone for dinner. Anyway, I'm pretty sure no saint is gonna miss a golden opportunity to meet Jesus and run,kick or scream to get out of his presence.

Disobedience can bring much pain and/or death.

Salvation is free, but walking with the Lord is costly (2 Tim 3:12 ESV). I'll take it though. I've come too far to turn back now.

This kind of sums it all up... y'all have to ask yourself Am I saved? (2 Corinthians 13:5 ESV) Can anyone see my light? (Matthew 5:16 KJV) If you're married to Jesus, act like it (Matthews 7:16 ESV).

If you're unsure of your salvation... one day it will be the last call (Hebrews 3:15 NIV). If you're only halfway sure then you're 100% lost. You can be unsure about anything, but please be sure of your final destination. Don't let the last call for salvation pass you by.

www.ingramcontent.com/pod-product-compliance
Lightning Source LLC
LaVergne TN
LVHW021051100526
838202LV00082B/5453